What Lovemaking
Means to
a Woman

What Lovemaking Means to a Woman

*Practical Advice
To Married Women
About Sex*

Tim and Beverly LaHaye

Zondervan Publishing House
Grand Rapids, Michigan

WHAT LOVEMAKING MEANS TO A WOMAN
Copyright © 1984 by The Zondervan Corporation

Zondervan Publishing House, 1415 Lake Drive, S.E.,
Grand Rapids, Michigan 49506

This book consists of two chapters taken from the larger book, *The Act
of Marriage*, copyright © 1976 by Tim and Beverly La Haye.

Library of Congress Cataloging in Publication Data
LaHaye, Tim F.
    What lovemaking means to a woman.

    Bibliography: p.
    1. Sex instruction for women.   2. Women—Sexual
behavior.   3. Sex in marriage.   4. Sex—Religious aspects—
Christanity.   I. LaHaye, Beverly.   II. Title.
HQ46.L26   1983   613.9'6   84-3545
ISBN 0-310-27052-9

Printed in the United States of America

    85   86   87   88   89   90 / 10   9   8   7   6   5   4   3

*To all those who believe married love
can be beautiful, exciting, and fulfilling
and to those who wish
they could believe*

Contents

Introduction

It is estimated that over 40 per cent of married women find their sex life unsatisfying. That is really sad because they have the same physical equipment as do the 60 per cent who enjoy it.

What is the problem? Either a lack of understanding of her intricate nature, a failure of her husband to understand her needs, or a lack of skill in the marriage bedroom.

This booklet contains three important chapters from our book *The Act of Marriage*, which God has used to help thousands of people. I am convinced that God never intended women to endure a second-rate sex life. In fact, we have received letters in our office—testimonials—to the effect that the principles in *The Act of Marriage* helped open the door to a beautiful love experience with their partner.

What most couples fail to understand is that lovemaking is an art that must be learned by two lovers. And the more each one knows about his partner and himself, the better equipped they will be to experience mutually satisfying physical love.

9

Many marriages only provide the husband with orgasmic satisfaction. That is not fatal to a marriage; neither, however, is it necessary.

This booklet will help both men and women understand what satisfying lovemaking means to a woman and better enable them to experience the joy of bringing pleasure to each other.

Author's note to inorgasmic wives: If you have never experienced an orgasm, or if you seldom do, you should consult chapters 8 and 9 in our book, *The Act of Marriage*, "The Unfulfilled Woman" and "The Key to Feminine Response."

1

The Art of Lovemaking

Every significant physical activity in life is learned by practice; why should lovemaking be different? Adult human beings possess the desire and necessary equipment to make love, but the art of lovemaking is learned — it is not innate.

Dr. Ed Wheat of Springdale, Arkansas, told a group of men in a seminar, "If you do what comes naturally in lovemaking, almost every time you will be wrong." In reality he was cautioning his male audience that each "natural" or self-satisfying step in gaining sexual gratification for a man would probably be incompatible with his wife's needs. For that reason, a couple must seriously study this subject just prior to marriage, and then after their marriage they can begin their practice to learn satisfying techniques.

It is unrealistic to expect two virgins to reach simultaneous climaxes on the first night of their honeymoon. Research indicates that nine out of ten brides do not experience orgasm in intercourse on the first attempt. Obviously it would be ridiculous for a couple to feel they had failed each other because they happened to be in the ninety percentile. It is much more realistic for a couple to recognize that they must "learn by doing." Isn't that the primary purpose of a honeymoon — for two lovebirds to get away to a romantic spot and learn about each other and their sexual natures?

When intercourse is an expression of love, it can be enjoyable even when one or both partners do not experience an orgasm. The tenderness and intimate relationship may prove to give sufficient satisfaction in themselves. Naturally one must expect intense stimulation ultimately to culminate in orgasm for both, but that goal is not usually achieved immediately. Such a rewarding skill is learned after study, experimentation, and open communication between husband and wife.

The art of love that exists well within the capabilities of every couple reading this book will be presented in this chapter for honeymooners, even though it will probably be read by more married veterans than newlyweds. After all, the difference in lovemaking between virgins and experienced married partners is minor. One marriage counselor has advised, "If couples would treat each other all through marriage as they do on their honeymoon, they would have very few sex problems. But most experienced couples try to take short cuts, and that is what spoils their potential satisfaction."

THE ULTIMATE GOAL

Many pleasurable side effects arise from lovemaking, but we should not lose sight of the fact that the ultimate objective is orgasm for both the husband and wife. For the man this is usually quite simple and easily detected. When sufficient stimulation is applied to the nerve endings in the glans penis, a chain reaction is begun by creating muscular contractions in the prostrate gland, forcing the milky seminal fluid and sperm cells through the urethra with a force strong enough to ejaculate as far as twenty-four inches. Only then does the man realize that almost every organ and gland in his body has been brought into action, for after orgasm they all start to relax, and he becomes overwhelmed with a feeling of contentment.

The woman's orgasm is much more complex, and since she seems to be capable of several levels of climax, it is less obvious. For that reason, many young wives aren't sure whether they have reached an orgasm or not. Just as the gentle art of love has to be learned, so must she discern by personal experience what to expect of an orgasm. Once she has achieved a high-level orgasm, no longer does she doubt what it is or when it occurs.

With the goal of mutual orgasm before them, a couple is advised to take whatever time and steps are necessary to achieve that objective. Love, patience, unselfishness, concentration, and persistence place that goal well within the capability of every married couple!

PREPARATION FOR LOVE

One young bride-to-be interrupted me during my usual talk on intimate relationships before marrying a couple. "Pastor LaHaye, do we have to talk about this? It embarrasses me. It will work out by itself." No wonder that naive young lady became pregnant during the first month of marriage, and I would be surprised if she has yet learned sexual satisfaction.

Fortunately most brides expect to enjoy lovemaking and realistically face the fact that some preparation is necessary before they begin the actual experience. All such young people would be advised to consider the following minimal steps in that preparation:

1. They should learn as much as they can before the wedding night. We feel that the reading of this book and others listed at the close of the chapter should not be reviewed together until after the wedding. But both bride and groom should read the basic material separate-

ly beforehand and then study it together on their honeymoon. This book is intended to be a help to such a couple on their wedding trip.

2. All prospective brides should visit their doctor several weeks before the wedding, discussing with him the advisability of breaking the hymen in the privacy of his office. If the doctor's examination shows that the hymen is thick and may obstruct sexual intercourse, she should consider letting him stretch it or cut it to avoid unnecessary pain and bleeding during intercourse. However, if the doctor feels she will have no serious difficulty and if the bride chooses, she may wish to leave it intact for her wedding night. In this enlightened age a bridegroom would rather have the hymen surgically removed in advance to reduce the possibility of causing pain to his virtuous young bride. Another alternative is digital stretching, which the husband can do on their wedding night, but this will require instructions from their doctor. In today's active world many virgins have broken the hymen in accidents while bicycling or horseback riding, or doctors may have had to dilate it because of menstrual difficulties.

The bride should discuss the matter of contraceptives with her doctor. It is important for the bride and groom to realize that the fear of pregnancy can seriously detract from the joy of a honeymoon. The young couple should know each other's feelings and decide whether they are prepared to start a family right after marriage or not. If they plan on a short delay, the doctor can advise them on a good, safe contraceptive.

3. It is a rare bride who will be able to provide sufficient natural vaginal lubricant on her honeymoon to avoid painful sensations during the act of love. This possibility can be eliminated by securing a tube of surgical jelly from the druggist, or she may wish to discuss this with her doctor, who can prescribe an adequate preparation for her. She would be advised to

have it handy for her husband to use at the proper time.

4. Every bride-to-be should familiarize herself with Dr. Kegel's exercise program that is found in chapter 9 of our book *The Act of Marriage*. The program is designed to acquaint her with muscle control, about which most women know nothing, and in addition will magnify her potential sexual feeling during lovemaking. It will also provide her with a means of exciting her husband beyond his fondest dreams. Learning these exercises will further assist them in learning to reach simultaneous orgasms.

PRELIMINARY CONSIDERATIONS

We have noted that most women are more romantic than men. "Women are incurably romantic" came the comment from one analyst. Instead of fighting against that fact, the wise husband will cooperate with this need in his wife's heart. Because the honeymoon is the culmination of a girl's lifetime dreams, a loving husband will make every effort to fulfill them.

When I look back on our honeymoon, I have to admit that I planned everything wrong. Bev and I were married on a Saturday night in her home church. An old friend and his wife who came to the wedding decided to join us at our apartment while he gave me a one-hour lecture on the "facts of life." This took place after the reception, pictures, and packing of our car. We went to bed at 1:45 A.M.! Our first married day was spent driving for twelve hours, then stopping about 8 P.M. in a motel room somewhere in the mountains of Kentucky. The next day we arrived in Greenville, South Carolina, where another ministerial student and I were building a trailer court for married students. I promptly went back to work. About the only clear lesson Bev learned from that hectic trip was to begin adjusting immediately to the insane pace to which I have subjected her for twenty-eight exciting years.

If I had known then what I know now, I would have planned those few days after the wedding differently. First, we would have been married in the afternoon. Then we would have slipped away from our friends to be alone, planning at least a week to get acquainted before my bride was confronted with her new life style as a wife.

One of the chief advantages of an afternoon wedding is having an entire first night without the fomenting turmoil that inevitably awaits a young couple after the reception. They need to get away to a hotel room to retire, unpack, freshen up, and leisurely enjoy a snack or dinner together. Most young people eat and sleep erratically before their wedding and, due to the frenzy of preparations, leave the ceremony totally exhausted. They need to sit down quietly, relax from all the excitement, and eat enough to lift their blood sugar level for added energy.

Upon returning to the room, the bridegroom may wish to carry his bride over the threshold in the traditional manner. From this point on, the two of them will be alone and should feel free to become as intimately acquainted as possible. The husband should proceed slowly and very gently with tender caresses and verbal expressions of love. There is a thin line at this stage between a husband's love and a man's passion. The husband who hurries this first encounter may unconsciously convey the thought to his new wife that he is being driven by passion more than love and concern for her. A slow, gentle approach will reveal his love for her through self-control.

It is important to add here that all lovemaking should proceed in circumstances where the couple can be guaranteed absolute privacy. Men are so single-minded that this is not so important to them as to their wives, but modest women need the assurance that no one will accidentally interrupt them. In a motel room it is easy to fasten the night lock. In their bedroom at home, they should install a lock on the door. Such a precaution is a necessary investment for successful lovemaking.

The romantic-minded husband will see to it that

lights are turned low, thus ensuring visibility without excessive brightness, and if possible provide soft music.

THE GREAT UNVEILING

At this point the husband must be very sensitive to the romantic fantasies of his wife. Some brides will succumb to the lingerie industry's commercials and wear a sexy nightie bought especially for the honeymoon. If so, she may want to slip into the bathroom to make the change. However, the couple may wish to stir sexual excitement for love by undressing one another. The lover finds it terribly exciting and stimulating to be gently undressed by his loved one. Although one may experience some embarrassment at being fully unclothed before his partner the first time, such a feeling will be minimal and will soon dissolve if the undressing proceeds slowly, even in stages, with tender, compassionate expressions of love. When the husband assures his modest bride that she is truly the most beautiful creature he has ever seen, she will most likely respond with a warm embrace.

FOREPLAY

Almost every sex manual emphasizes the need for an adequate period of foreplay, or loveplay. This is true not only on the first night, but all through marriage. Most men have learned that foreplay is essential to their wives' enjoyment of lovemaking, but they generally minimize their own need because they are fully aroused for lovemaking at the sight of their beloved's nude body. Yet current research has revealed that it is easier for a man to retard his ejaculation after a long period of foreplay than after sudden arousal. Besides, as he learns how affectionately to arouse his wife, he will attain in her response intense excitement himself, and it will enrich his own climax.

How long the couple should spend in foreplay may vary with each couple's need, depending somewhat upon their temperaments and cultural background. But it is never wise to be in a hurry. A modest, inexperienced bride may require thirty or more minutes in preparation for lovemaking. After she becomes more experienced, the preparatory time may be reduced to ten or fifteen minutes; occasional exceptions during her emotional cycle when she is particularly amorous may reduce the time even further.

There is no universal pattern for arousing a woman to lovemaking. Some women are stimulated by having their breasts caressed, others are not. Furthermore, a woman's emotional cycle may make it enjoyable for her on some occasions, but not on others. For this reason, a wife should freely instruct her husband through verbal responses and by placing his hands where she wants him to caress her tenderly. Generally a thoughtful husband may gently massage his wife's neck, shoulders, and breasts to arouse her until blood rushes to the nipples and they become firm and erect, though care should be taken not to irritate the nipples by too vigorous action. Any tender fondling and kissing on the upper body will help to arouse her. Gradually the husband should move his hands gently down his wife's body until he contacts the vulva region, mindful to keep his fingernails smoothly filed to avoid producing any discomfort (which could cause her heating emotions to become suddenly chilled).

As the husband is tenderly caressing the clitoris or vaginal area with his hand, the couple will probably be lying on the bed with the wife on her back. If she will spread her legs, keeping her feet flat on the bed, and pull them up toward her body, it will be helpful for them both. The husband finds this voluntary act of cooperation very exciting, and it makes her most sensitive areas accessible to his caressing fingers. It is best for the husband to fondle the area around the clitoris, but he should not start foreplay there at first because of potential irritation. As the area

18

starts to engorge with blood, it becomes the primary source of excitement to the wife and is then ready for direct stimulation.

On first arousal the husband will be able to feel the clitoris with his fingers, but his wife will go through several physiological changes as her excitement mounts. Her heart will palpitate, her skin become warm, and almost every part of her body become sensitive to the touch. Her breathing will be more rapid, her face may grimace as if in pain, and she may groan audibly — and her husband finds this all very exhilarating. The most noticeable change will take place in the vaginal area, where she becomes very moist and the inner lips (labia minora) begin to swell several times their normal size until they form a hood over the clitoris, which may no longer be felt by his fingers. At this point it usually becomes unnecessary to maintain direct contact with the clitoris, for any motion in the vaginal region will vibrate against the thick layers of the swollen hood and transmit the movements to the clitoris indirectly. This will further amplify passion in the wife.

The vigor with which the husband massages this vital area should be determined by the wife. Some prefer it slow and easy, while others enjoy vigorous motion. Some wives like to vary the motion within one lovemaking experience; others may choose to modify it according to their mood. Most important, the husband should be extremely gentle and sensitive to his wife's needs at this point.

The mounting passions and tensions in a wife at this stage can be likened to pushing a cart uphill. As one gradually approaches the top, the peak seems to become steeper; then with a final thrust, the cart can be pushed over the top. Just as one would never stop the cart on the uphill side, so a thoughtful husband will not suspend his motion in the midst of their loveplay. If he does, her emotional cart will *immediately* descend and he will have to regain the emotional loss. This explains why many women cool somewhat during the time it takes a husband to remove his fingers from her vaginal area and place his penis inside, particularly if he has any clothing to remove. With practice he can learn to continue the massaging loveplay while putting the penis into place. This will help his wife continue her climb toward a high emotional peak. After the husband learns more self-control, he may stimulate his wife's clitoris with a lubricated penis. Some wives may prefer this to the husband's fingers. Then it is easily slipped into the vagina when she is ready.

THE CULMINATION

Many an inexperienced husband misunderstands a very important signal from his wife. When his fingers are caressing the vaginal area and he finds it well lubricated, he may consider that to be the signal that she is ready for coitus. This is not true!! Until her labia minora are heavily swollen by the influx of an ample supply of blood, the sensitive areas of her vagina will not even be included in their lovemaking. If he proceeds before that, he will probably reach orgasm just as this swelling takes place, and she will be left unfulfilled. His relaxing penis will then be unable to continue the motion on the sides of the vagina and the clitoris necessary to bring her to climax. This common misunderstanding probably has kept more loving partners from learning to reach simultaneous orgasms than anything else.

The husband must also remember when massaging the area of the vagina and clitoris that at first touch with dry fingers his wife might experience some discomfort. If he moistens his finger with vaginal lubrication, she will find clitoral stimulation much more enjoyable. Free and honest communication is essential in this phase of loveplay to maximize the enjoyment of this necessary preparation for the act of marriage.

Several writers in this field, both Christian and secular suggest that a couple gently massage each other to orgasm on their wedding night for two reasons: (1) it increases the possibility for both to experience an orgasm the first night, and (2) it helps to acquaint them with their partner's bodily functions. We believe this might be a little too much to expect from two inhibited virgins their first night together. We suggest, however, that they arouse each other as outlined above, and when the wife thinks she is ready for entrance, she should take the groom's penis in her hand and place it in her vagina. Upon his wife's signal and while continuing to massage her clitoral area, the husband should use his free hand to take a lubricating jelly (which should be placed on the nightstand in advance) and lubricate the head and shaft of his penis before entrance. He should be careful to support the weight of his body with his elbows and slowly push his penis into her vagina.

Once inside, the husband should try to remain motionless or he may ejaculate in a matter of seconds, abruptly terminating their lovemaking. Even though all his instincts cry out within him to begin his thrusting motion, he must gain self-control for at least one or two minutes. To avoid the loss of his wife's mounting tension, he should continue to massage her clitoral area or the swollen lips of the vulva. The wife can help to increase her passion by slightly rotating her hips as she lies beneath her husband. This helps to maintain motion and friction on her clitoris and bring her vagina into contact with the shaft of his penis without overstimulating him. When she feels her passions mounting beyond control, she should put her legs around her husband's hips and begin her own thrusting movements back and forth on the penis. If she has practiced contracting the vaginal (P.C.) muscle several weeks before marriage, she will find more pleasure in the experience and can help her husband by squeezing his penis with the muscle each time he retracts. A squeezing action upon first entry is also helpful to both husband and wife — while the husband is waiting one to two minutes for ejaculatory control, his wife's squeezing can maintain her exitement. Once the husband begins his thrusting motion, the wife should concentrate on the sensations she is experiencing in her clitoris and vaginal area, continuing as much motion as possible that contributes to that feeling.

The husband, no matter how inexperienced, will intuitively recognize his wife's accelerated motion as the signal for him to begin his thrusting motion, and he will likely expel his mixture of seminal fluid and sperm cells into her vagina within just a few thrusts. He should continue thrusting after his ejaculation as long as he can in case his wife's orgasm is all but seconds behind his.

Shortly after ejaculation, his penis will lose its rigidity and will no longer maintain sufficient friction on the vagina walls and labia minora to increase his wife's excitement. If she has not reached an orgasm during their first coitus, the young lovers should not feel discouraged. The husband can immediately begin manual stimulation of his wife's clitoris and vulva area, as he did in foreplay, to help bring her to orgasm. Although it is possible for a bride to experience orgasm during the couple's first encounter, it is unusual, especially for a virgin.

THE AFTERGLOW

Most brides find their initial lovemaking, when preceded by sufficient loveplay, a delightfully exciting experience even without orgasm. The free experimentation with their beloved's nude body is stimulating, unsurpassed by any previous experience. Even such pain as she may have felt in the breaking of her hymen or the possible stretching of the vagina will usually be eclipsed by the stimulation of areas she has never used before. Many wives have indicated that the blast of their lover's warm seminal fluid inside the vagina is also thrilling. Coupled with the intimate closeness of their entwined bodies, this makes it a most enjoyable expression of love. If her orgasm was not achieved, her emotional tension will gradu-

22

ally subside and her reproductive organs, like those of her husband, will slowly return to normal.

There is no need for lovers to withdraw immediately after completion of intercourse. We advise that they remain in each other's embrace for several minutes and continue to exchange caresses. Many couples fall asleep in this position or learn to roll onto their sides, the limp penis gradually sliding out of the vagina. Their physical and emotional exhaustion generally produces a deep, satisfying slumber.

It usually takes the husband forty-five minutes to an hour or more before he can be ready for lovemaking again. This is not true of the wife. Research by Masters and Johnson indicates that a woman can experience several orgasms, one right after another.[1] For that reason, whenever a wife is brought to orgasm by her husband's hand during foreplay, he should continue to massage her vaginal and clitoral area, for she will soon regain the feeling of mounting excitement and can repeat the orgasmic experience. It may be difficult for a man to understand how his wife can immediately be ready for more when he is powerless to regain his sex drive without a period of rest, but she is suprisingly capable of continuing orgasms. In fact, some women have reported that their most powerful climaxes are sometimes their fourth or fifth in a lovemaking session. However, if the husband stops his stimulation of the clitoris and vaginal area immediately after the first orgasm, she will gradually lose her mounting passion and retreat to a state of emotional and physical exhaustion similar to that of her husband.

HONEYMOON EXPERIMENTATION

Honeymoons exist not only to provide a special time for companionship, but to promote sexual learning and experimentation. For that reason, couples should try various methods of stimulation, positions, times of day, and whatever they both find enjoyable. We recommend that sometime during their honeymoon, in order to understand fully their partner's physiological function during lovemaking, they bring each other to orgasm by hand. This experiment should be carried out in a lighted room where they may be free from any interruptions. Unclothed, they should maintain the same romantic atmosphere and unhurried preparation as for any other period of lovemaking.

It is advisable that the husband try to bring his wife to orgasm first, because after his climax it is usually difficult for him to be vitally interested in lovemaking for some time. Proceeding in the manner outlined above, he should lie on his side next to and slightly above his wife while he tenderly caresses the clitoris and the vaginal area with his hand. When the labia minora are sufficiently swollen, indicating that she is responding properly and her vagina is well lubricated, he will feel that the protective hood has covered the clitoris area, and he can create friction in both places at once. She may want him to insert one finger very gently into the vagina, making slow rhythmic movements inside while his other fingers continue contact with the outer vulval area. This will usually give her a delightful sensation and help to increase her excitement. She should feel free to use her hand to guide her husband's to the most responsive areas and create the most stimulating motions. Then she should concentrate with abandon on those vital areas of friction and let herself go completely, so that if she wishes to groan, cry, wiggle, rotate, or thrust, she may do so.

To realize fully her capability after her first orgasm, the wife should encourage her husband to slacken his motions, but not discontinue them. As her excitement begins to mount again, she can signal him to speed up his motion and increase its vigor to her satisfaction until she reaches another orgasm. Twice will probably be sufficient at this state of their marriage.

After her climax, the wife should turn on her side while the husband lies on his back. Gently massaging the genital region, she should run her fingers over his penis, pubic hair, scrotum, and inner thighs. She should be very careful not to put pressure on his testicles located inside his scrotal sac, as this can be quite uncomfortable. With her hand around the shaft of the penis, she should begin massaging up and down. As her motion becomes more rapid, her husband's body will grow more rigid, and she will be able to verify his response to her touch. This motion should be continued until he ejaculates. Before beginning this exercise, the wife should have several tissues on hand to absorb the discharge. Afterward she can observe how rapidly her husband's penis returns to normal.

Dr. Herbert J. Miles, in his excellent book *Sexual Happiness in Marriage*, tells the following story:

> One couple in the research sample had this experience. They attempted intercourse on their wedding night and the wife did not have an orgasm, but the husband did. After intercourse, they attempted to bring her to an orgasm by direct stimulation. In the process she gradually became tense, nervous, and just could not continue the arousal effort, although she tried and wanted to do so. She had to ask her husband to stop the stimulation. They lay there, relaxed, and talked for over three hours, on into the night. Finally, long after midnight she said, "I want us to try that again." They repeated the process of direct stimulation and after about seventeen minutes she reached her first orgasm. What actually happened, in her case, was that she learned much in her first effort and after becoming relaxed and more confident, she was able to give herself fully to sexual arousal and thus succeeded.[2]

Some Christians might object to this form of experimentation. We recommend it for newlyweds, because they are building a lifetime relationship together in which lovemaking will play a permanent role for up to sixty years. The more they know about each other by personal experience, the more they will enjoy each other and more likely experience what we consider the ultimate in lovemaking: simultaneous orgasms most of the time. This form of "learning by doing" will increase the likelihood that they will learn the art early in marriage and go on to enjoy it for many years. Part of the therapy recommended by Masters and Johnson for sexual dysfunction is this same experimentation. Couples married for years have been helped to a better understanding of each other and a better sexual relationship through this kind of learning process.

Dr. Miles suggests, "There are three steps in sexual adjustment that couples need to learn. They are as follows: first step — orgasms, second step — orgasms in intercourse, third step — orgasms together or close together in intercourse."[3]

A couple should not be discouraged if they do not achieve the second or third step right away. It may take several weeks or longer before they can experience simultaneous orgasms on a regular basis. However, it should be a goal for which every couple strives.

Another area in which a couple will want to experiment is positions for most effective sexual arousal. One of the most convenient has the wife lying on her back with knees bent and feet pulled up to her hips and her husband lying on her right side. Dr. Miles explains what the Bible says about a married couple's position for lovemaking.

This position of sexual arousal is described in the Bible in the Song of Solomon 2:6 and 8:3. These two verses are identical. They read as follows: "Let his left hand be under my head and his right hand embrace me." The word "embrace" could be translated "fondle" or "stimulate." Here in the Bible, in a book dealing with pure married love, a married woman expresses herself with longing that her husband put his left arm under her head and that he uses his right hand to stimulate her clitoris.

This position of sexual arousal seems to have been the position used by many people back through the centuries. We do not hesitate to say that the general arousal procedure described here is a part of the plan of God as

He created man and woman. Therefore, mankind has used this procedure because it is the plan of God and because it is efficient.[4]

Dr. Miles further gives some sound advice regarding the extent of intimacy between the husband and wife.

> In interpersonal relationships in the community and society, modesty is a queen among virtues, but in the privacy of the marriage bedroom, behind locked doors, and in the presence of pure married love, there is no such thing as modesty. A couple should feel free to do whatever they both enjoy which moves them into a full expression of their mutual love and in a sexual experience.
> At this point it is well to give a word of caution. *All sex experiences should be those which both husband and wife want.* Neither, at any time, should force the other to do anything that he does not want to do. Love does not force.[5]

One characteristic of the Holy Spirit is love, and a dominant trait of love is kindness. The intimacy of lovemaking should always be performed with kindness. At times vigorous activity is required, but it will always be expressed in kindness to the other person — a vital evidence that the act of marriage is in reality an act of love.

CLITORAL STIMULATION

The reluctance of many loving partners to incorporate clitoral stimulation as a necessary and meaningful part of their foreplay has probably cheated more women out of the exciting experience of orgasmic fulfillment than any other one thing. Because it has often been associated with self-stimulation, even some husbands are unaware of how essential a part of the lovemaking process it is.

To highlight the significance of the clitoris to the woman's sexual enjoyment, many researchers have compared it with the penis. It has been called the "most keenly sexual part of a woman's body" and is still regarded by many "as the seat of all sexual satisfaction."[6]

R.M. Deutsch has stated that "stimulation of the clitoris alone will produce an orgasm in nearly all women . . . . direct clitoral stimulation alone [will] produce the climax."[7] He further indicates that "most researchers agree that the clitoris, unlike any male organ, has only one purpose — sexual stimulation."[8]

Another researcher indicates that the clitoris has the same number of nerve endings as does the penis, but is only one-tenth the size. Therefore it is the culmination in feminine sexual capability. To disregard it is to guarantee feminine orgasmic malfunction or incapability.

From a practical standpoint it has no bearing on reproduction and is unnecessary for any other female function. Thus it is safe to conclude that God designed it to be used in lovemaking. It could well be that the thrilling response of the wife referred to in the Song of Solomon 5:4 may allude to the husband's use of clitoral manipulation. Such foreplay is not only acceptable behavior by married partners, but also was designed by God as one of the most delightful aspects of the act of marriage.

THE FOUR PHASES OF SEXUAL AROUSAL

Modern research, particularly that of Masters and Johnson, acquaints us with four distinct phases of sexual arousal for both male and female: (1) the excitement phase, (2) the plateau phase, (3) the orgasmic phase, and (4) the resolution phase. Admittedly, reducing all human responses to a single chart does not allow for individual variation, and from that standpoint it oversimplifies the matter, but it does provide a basic pattern upon which to establish a norm. As noted in the following diagrams, only one characteristic response of men is indicated, whereas three are listed for women. The male response is more prone to be basic, whereas women tend to reflect more individual variation. In addition, because of the greater complexity of a woman's orgasmic function, she may experience each of these responses throughout

Fig. 3. Sexual response of the husband

her married life as she is learning the art of love expression.

On the wife's chart we have distinguished the three responses as (A) the multiple orgasm, the ideal she would like to achieve; (B) the orgasmic failure, the sexual response that far too many settle for (a failure that often can be changed by a little more understanding, added foreplay, and increased tenderness on the part of her companion; and (C) the single orgasm, probably the most frequent expression of the well-adjusted married woman who may reserve the multiple experience for special occasions when her mood, time allotted for lovemaking, and other factors fall into place.

Fig. 4 Sexual response of the wife

As the chart indicates a certain physiological changes take place in each stage. These should be studied and lovers should experiment to the point of learning what to expect in each of these phases.

VARIOUS POSITIONS

Since the earliest days of writing various lovemaking positions have been recorded. One author claims there are ninety-nine different positions. The trouble with about ninety-five of them is that only a gymnast could enjoy them. Actually there are only four positions used frequently enough to consider here. Dr. Miles shares his research findings on the first three.

1. *The husband above*

Our research indicates that 91 percent of couples use the man above position all of the time or most all of the time. Fifty-four percent of couples experiment frequently with other positions, but usually finish with the man above position. Only 4 percent use some position other than the man above position more than half of the time, and only 5 percent use some other position all of the time.

It is important to the husband to have his feet firmly against the foot of the bed or some solid object to aid him in giving full expression to his sexual orgasm. In case of a bed that has no foot-board, the couple may reverse their position, placing his feet against the head-board.

2. *The wife above*

The wife above position allows the husband to relax and control himself, and permits the wife to initiate the movement necessary to give her the most stimulation by forcing the clitoris to move over the penis. The disadvantages are that this position is often not comfortable for the wife, the husband may have difficulty in controlling his arousal, and neither are in proper position to give fullest expression during orgasms. For some couples the advantages outweigh the disadvantages. This position is often advantageous for a large husband and a small wife.

3. *Both on their sides*

Another useful position is for both husband and wife to lie on their sides facing the same direction with the husband back of the wife. The penis is moved into the vaginal passage from the rear. The disadvantages are that the penis cannot contact the clitoris and the couple cannot kiss during the experience. The advantages are that the position is very comfortable, the husband can easily use his fingers to stimulate his wife's clitoris, and he can control his own arousal. There are other slight variations of this approach. Many couples use this position for the arousal period and shift quickly to the man above position for orgasms.[9]

4. *Husband seated.*

Depending on their comparative heights, a couple may sometimes enjoy the position of the husband seated on a low couch or backless chair. The wife can lower herself onto his penis at her discretion. This position is good for those wives who find that the entrance of the male organ is painful. By controlling the entrance, a wife can minimize the pain. Such sensations will be short-lived, and couples should not give up or use pain as an excuse to avoid lovemaking permanently. If pain is not eliminated by application of generous amounts of lubricant, see your physician.

Most couples experiment with these and other positions, but most return to the man above. It seems to be the most satisfying to the largest number of lovers.

SUMMARY

The art of mutually enjoyable lovemaking is not difficult to learn, but neither is it automatic. No one is a good lover by nature, and thus the more selfish the individual, the more difficulty he will have learning this art. If two people love each other with an unselfish love and are willing to control themselves while seeking to learn how to render emotional and physical satisfaction to their partner, they will learn. It does, however, demand time and practice. Any individual taking time to read this book has indicated he is concerned enough to try. Dr. Ed Wheat has sagely said, "Every physical union should be a contest to see which partner can outplease the other."

With this concept in mind, I told a story in the chapter on "Physical Adjustment" in my book *How to Be Happy Though Married*. It was given to me by a minister friend who had counseled a frustrated couple in the art of clitoral stimulation so that in a very brief period of time they resolved their problem.

Four months after that book was published, I was speaking at a banquet in a very small city in northern California. A dentist shared with me privately that he had read the book and had been reminded of his own case. When he related his story, I found it an exciting corollary to the earlier tale.

The young dentist and his wife of three years were deeply in love, but his wife had never reached orgasm during their marriage. He found this almost as frustrating as she did. As a dentist, he had studied anatomy and felt that he knew more than the average person about the functions of the human body. This knowledge, however, did not seem to resolve their difficulty, and their sexual frustration soon produced marital conflict. Since they were not Christians at the time, they decided to start going to church as a last resort to save their marriage. They fortunately selected a gospel-preaching church, and in about three months they both had accepted Christ as their personal Lord and Savior. But this still did not resolve their problem of orgasmic malfunction.

One Sunday morning their pastor was preaching on the text, "In all thy ways acknowledge Him, and He shall direct thy paths." They heard him say, "You do not have a problem in your life that you cannot take to the Lord in prayer." The dentist looked at his wife and realized that they had not prayed about it. Afterward they discussed it and decided to do so.

On Friday of that week they were invited to a social gathering. Being the first to arrive, they were ushered into the family room to await the arrival of the other guests. It was a large room with a couple of conversation areas, so they chose a couch on the far side of the room. They were no sooner seated than another couple came in and sat on the first couch behind them, a large floral arrangement preventing them from being seen by the new arrivals. Thinking they were alone, this sanguine husband put his arm around his wife and exclaimed, "Hasn't our relationship been beautiful since we discovered clitoral stimulation?" The dentist silently glanced at his wife and thought, "We have never tried that." That night they did, and it was the beginning of a new experience for them both.

With obvious emotion the dentist told me, "That simple technique was like a key that opened the door to a beautiful relationship which we have enjoyed for the past three years."

This story shows evidence of God's abundant grace. In a small town without counselors, and under the ministry of a young, single seminary student, this young couple told their heavenly Father of their need and sought His help. He guided them to the right place at the right time to hear the information He wanted them to know.

No one has a problem that cannot be taken to his heavenly Father. No one need settle for a lifetime of sexual frustration. When God's children pray for His guidance and His will for their lives, He is always faithful in revealing it to them. This relationship with God will bless the lives and strengthen the faith of those who trust in Him for help.

Notes

[1] William H. Masters and Virginia E. Johnson, *Human Sexual Response* (Boston: Little, Brown and Co., 1966), p. 131.

[2] Herbert J. Miles, *Sexual Happiness in Marriage* (Grand Rapids: Zondervan Publishing House, 1967), p. 96.

[3] Ibid., p. 97.

[4] Ibid., p. 79.

[5] Ibid., p. 78.

[6] Ronald M. Deutsch, *The Key to Feminine Response in Marriage* (New York: Random House, 1968), p. 39.

2

What Lovemaking Means
to a Woman

Fortunately for women, men and cultures are changing! It is reported that a generation ago many men appeared to be selfish lovers and society helped contribute to the "he-man" self-images that made them seem like animals in the bedroom. Sexual pleasure from "the little woman" was assumed to be their divine right, and their relations were usually one-sided experiences that left an affectionate wife with the frustrated feeling that she had been used, not loved.

Such men were (and some still are) sexual illiterates, totally failing to comprehend a woman's emotional or physical needs. Assuming that he had the gift of intuitive knowledge in this department, a man took his innocent bride to their love nest and taught her only what she needed to know to satisfy *his* sex drive.

It is no wonder that many wives grew to be frigid and lovemaking turned into a chore. Even worse, some frustrated wives became evangelists of frigidity. Consequently young brides went into marriage dutifully warned that homemaking, motherhood, and a good reputation were wonderful — but the one drawback to marriage was the "bedroom scene."

The modern Christian husband has been challenged by the Word of God and his pastor, "Husbands, love your wives, even as Christ also loved the church. . . . So ought men to love their wives as their own bodies" (Eph. 5:25, 28). Thus a Christian man today enters marriage more sensitive to the love needs of his bride and more concerned with her satisfaction. He respects her as a special creation of God who should be accepted and understood. During the past decade several books on marriage dealing quite frankly with the subject have given man a greater understanding of woman. Unless his head remains in the sand, he can learn many things about her. And the more he knows about her, the more he can tailor his affectionate passions to her emotional needs.

A sage once said, "A woman is the most complex creature on earth." Certainly no reasonable man would claim to understand her fully. However, after dealing with hundreds of these delicate creatures in the privacy of the counseling room, my wife and I have discovered to a greater extent what the act of marriage means to a woman. Every man can profit from reading this chapter; the more a husband knows about his wife's erotic needs and what the act of marriage truly means to her, the more he and his wife together can enjoy each other, not only physically but in every other area of life.

Let us consider these five significant areas that show what lovemaking means to a woman:

1. *It fulfills her womanhood.* Self-image psychology is the rage today. Every bookstand carries several self-help publications, and many are best sellers. We Christians do not agree with all their humanistic conclusions, but we certainly cannot deny the important truth that lasting happiness is impossible until a person learns to accept himself. This is true of a married woman. If she considers herself unsuccessful in bed, she will have a difficult time accepting her total womanhood.

It should not come as a surprise that almost every bride feels insecure when she marries. From ages eighteen to twenty-five few people are secure. It often takes from one-third to one-half of a lifetime for folks really to accept themselves. Naturally, being a Spirit-filled Christian contributes to a good self-image, but marriage is one of the most important decisions a person makes in life; consequently any normal person will face it with a degree of trepidation. If a major part of married life proves unsatisfactory, it complicates self-image. Not incidentally, we have yet to counsel a frigid woman with a good self-image.

One way to understand the function of the female mind is to contrast it with the male thought system. A man has the God-given mandate to be the provider of the family. Consequently his mental psyche is so oriented that he gains much of his self-image from successful occupational pursuits. That is the reason a man's goals and dreams take a vocational tack early in life. Ask a junior-age boy what he wants to be when he grows up and he will usually reply a fireman, policeman, doctor, baseball player, or jet pilot. Although he changes that goal several times as he matures, it does indicate his vocational psyche. Ask a little girl what she wants to be when she becomes a woman and she will usually answer "a mother" or "housewife." In adulthood and even after thorough vocational training, many women still list the role of homemaker as their main vocational objective.

When in Jackson, Mississippi, for a Family Life Seminar, I was interviewed by a young woman reporter. It took only a moment to detect her hostility arising from the humiliation of having to interview a minister. Most newspapers assign cub reporters to the religion desk, as in her case. Obviously she would rather have been assigned to someone "important." Accepting her hostility as a challenge, I decided to break through her tough veneer of professionalism by asking her the question I have presented to scores of people as I travel around the country. I had previously learned that she was a journalism major in college, determined to be the "best reporter in the state."

I also discovered that because of an unfortunate love affair at the age of twenty-two, she "hated" men. When she finally became a little friendlier, I began, "I'm taking an informal survey. Would you mind if I ask you a personal question?"

Every curious woman responds affirmatively to that approach. I continued, "What is the one thing you want most out of life?"

She deliberated a moment and replied, "A home and a family."

Somewhat teasingly I asked, "And a husband?"

She blushed a little and said softly, "I guess so."

Even I was a bit surprised to find a woman whose external facade identified her with the philosophy of the women's liberation movement confessing the natural longing of every woman's heart — to be a homemaker.

This intuitive tendency is, in our opinion, the primary drive in a woman. She should never be ashamed of this psychical phenomenon; God made her this way. The most frustrated women in the world are those who stifle or substitute that tendency for a lesser priority. If our assumption is true, and we believe it is, then her rating as a wife is all-important to a woman.

You may be asking, "What relation does that have to the act of marriage?" Everything! A wife is more than a mother and homemaker. She is also a sexual partner to her mate. Like the male, if she does not succeed in the bedroom, she fails in other areas — for two reasons: first, few men accept bedroom failure without being carnal, nasty, and insulting; second and more important, if her husband doesn't enjoy her lovemaking, he will make his disapproval obvious. A woman receives major portions of her self-esteem from her husband. In fact, we have yet to find a woman with a good self-image who disapproves of herself as a wife. This, in our opinion, is one reason divorcees often marry beneath themselves the second time — they have been beaten down by their husbands and forfeited the self-acceptance that is vital to everyone.

An anxious woman came for counseling to ask my opinion as to whether she or her husband was right. "I think sex is unnecessary in a Christian marriage. My husband doesn't agree." Sexually well-adjusted women and all men would side with her husband, but our research indicates that some sexually frustrated women would agree with her. This lady dogmatically announced, "I can live the rest of my life without sex!" Is it any wonder that she ranks as the married woman with the lowest self-image we have ever counseled? When confronted with the challenge that she would never learn to accept herself as a woman unless her husband accepted her as a wife, she returned to her marriage bed with a new motivation. In time and with God's help, that new attitude transformed both their relationship and her personality. Today she is a mature woman with a reasonably good self-image.

2. *It reassures her of her husband's love.* The one point on which psychologists agree is that all people have a basic need to be loved. This is generally more true of women than men. Women have a tremendous capacity for love, both giving and receiving. Hundreds of illustrations could be given of "mother-love," "wife-love," or "sister-love," but the reader is doubtlessly familiar with these already. However, many are unaware of the five kinds of love required by a woman.

(a) *Companionship love.* Few women enjoy solitude for long periods of time. Have you noticed how few hermits and recluses are women? A few exceptions may be found among the aged, of course, when women become senile or have outlived all their loved ones. But a woman looks upon marriage as perpetual companionship, which explains why so many marital problems occur when a man's job takes him out of the home for long periods of time. Too often he does not understand this need for companionship in his wife. When he is regularly surrounded by people, he usually can't wait to get away for a while and be alone. When he arrives home, he may find his wife craving his attention and company.

If men realized this need in their wives, they would spend less time in front of the television set when they are at home and learn to enjoy wifely companionship. It is also true that many women would do well to improve their companionship appeal by talking about things that interest men instead of making small talk. It is unwise for a wife to direct all the conversation toward her interests when her husband comes home. It is a good rule to accompany his arrival home with pleasant conversation that is interesting to him and conveys a message of love and welcome. This usually involves allowing him to share his thoughts with her and showing her interest in his activities. This gives her opportunities to build him up with her positive comments.

Couples seldom have problems being good companions before marriage, but if they fail to cultivate that relationship, they seem to lose it. In a letter to his mother nine months after he was married, our son wrote, "Kathy is my best friend." He didn't realize it, but he was claiming companionship love for his bride.

It is often hard for a woman to give physical love to a man who does not return her companionship love. It is always easier to give love when it is needed and appreciated by the receiver. A good wife must know that her husband needs her companionship just as she requires his, no matter how successful or busy he may be. In fact, the more prosperous he is in his vocation, the more she needs his companionship.

(b) *Compassionate love.* A woman has a natural bedside manner, but only a few men display that kind of compassion. When a child or husband hurts, who runs to his aid? Who jumps out of bed at 2:30 A.M. at the slightest whimper of the baby? Rarely the baby's father! A mother does not manifest compassionate love because she is a mother, but because she is a woman.

Men need to learn that a woman's capacity for compassionate love testifies to her need to receive it also. That is especially true when she is suffering emotionally or physically. It is regrettable that the man who enjoys her compassionate love when he hurts is often slow to return it to his loving wife. The Golden Rule is quite applicable here.

(c) *Romantic love.* Women are romantics! Lurking in the heart of every girl (even when she is grown up) is the image of prince charming on his white horse coming to wake up the beautiful princess with her first kiss of love. For that reason she needs romance, flowers, music, soft lights, dinner out, and a host of other things. Unfortunately many a man fails to understand that, primarily because his need for romantic love is either nonexistent or minimal. But he is married to a creature with an extraordinary need for romance. Some men misjudge their wives, deeming them more practical minded than other women. To be truthful, these wives have likely tried to overcome that "dream" by becoming practical; to these women it seems better to suppress that desire than to become disappointed over the lack of romanticism in their husbands. However, an occasional night out without the children, some little unexpected gift, or another expression of "romance" can be very rewarding to her.

This difference between men and women may contribute to feelings of incompatibility after marriage. A woman never loses the need to be romanced, whereas a man doesn't even possess that need. His emotions are near the surface and easily ignited; hers are deep and burn slowly. It is this romantic love that makes a woman respond to her husband's little expressions of thoughtfulness like opening the car door, taking her arm as she crosses the street, or expressing the "Sir Walter Raleigh routine." He may sometimes feel a bit foolish, but her response is worth the abashment.

I remember driving up in front of the church one Sunday. Five men were watching as I walked around the car and opened the door for Beverly. Frankly, I felt self-conscious, but she made it all worthwhile, not only by the little squeeze on my hand as we walked into church, but also later that night. After preaching five times that day, I was exhausted as we pulled into the driveway. It was about eleven o'clock and was raining lightly. As I pulled on the emergency brake, I was amazed to hear her door open and see her run around in front of the headlights to lift the double garage door. What made her do it? At five o'clock she had a romantic need to be honored and preferred in front of our friends; at eleven o'clock she showed her appreciation and responded to my need.

Don't be tricked into thinking that today's "mod" women are any different, just because some of them wear frumpy clothes and sometimes act as if they care little about manners and etiquette. Something deep down in a woman's heart cries out for romantic love.

Jeri is a case in point. At twenty-one she was led to Christ by a young woman in our church with whom she had gone to high school. When she first started attending services, she wore blue jeans and a white T-shirt. Outwardly she was somewhat coarse and very independent. As she grew in her faith in the Lord, she began to dress up and fix her hair. Surprisingly she proved to be a very attractive young woman. Before long Roy met her, asked to meet her parents, and started dating her. About a year later Jeri came into my office to discuss wedding plans. When I asked what she liked about Roy, she replied, "He treats me like a lady. He's the first fellow who ever came up to the door to pick me up for a date or opened the car door or seated me at the table." When I asked how she liked that kind of treatment, her eyes filled with tears as she whispered, "I love it!" She had dated boys for about seven years, but the first one to treat her like a lady won her heart. The reason is simple: women need romantic love.

(d) *Affectionate love.* Most women crave kisses of appreciation. You perhaps are acquainted with some exceptions — so are we — but if you look deeper you will find that such lack of affection has been learned. It is sometimes caused by a husband who demands quick sex instead of slow lovemaking. Some inconsiderate men can be satisfied with that, but almost all women are not. To them a tender touch, a warm embrace, and the closeness of one they love is almost as enjoyable as the more intimate contact. In fact, many wives respond to an approving look and words of commendation. It is a wise husband who breaks out of the routine frequently to voice approval of his wife. Such men do not testify to sexual starvation, for they have learned that their wives are ignited by the little expressions of affection that often seem meaningless to a man.

Personally I care not a bit for flowers. If we never had them in our home, I wouldn't miss them. But almost every time I return from a seminar on a Saturday night, I pick up a bouquet of roses for Bev in the San Diego airport. Why? Because I like the response they create in her. Frankly, it took several years to learn the rewards of conforming my behavior to her need for affection. She not only likes yellow roses, but is grateful that I was thinking of her as I came into town.

(e) *Passionate love*. Impassioned love comes naturally to a man because of his stronger sex drive. Most women have to cultivate the appetite for passionate loving, but be sure of this — they have the capacity to learn. The husband who confers affectionate love upon his mate can teach her passionate love. And any man who has done so will testify that it is time well invested.

As we will see, a woman's passions are more periodic than a man's. On occasions, given the right place, privacy, and quality of affection, she can thoroughly enjoy passionate love. Yet one thing should be remembered: It is easier for a woman to express passionate love after the other four needs for love have been satisfied.

When these love needs in a woman's heart have been properly fulfilled, they will give assurance of her husband's love, which is becoming increasingly important in an era when men and women mingle together day after day in the business world. Many a married man is surrounded by secretaries or other employees whose physical allurements are on display during working hours. When a husband is confronted by another woman who happens to be on his wavelength, the best safeguard against moral problems is a warm love relationship with his wife. "Male eroticism, fulfilled within the home, does not hunger for more outside."[1] That is also true of the wife. Since she needs to know that her husband needs her, lovemaking becomes a necessary means of reassuring her of that love.

This yearning for reassurance was beautifully shared by a close friend, whose lovely wife had incurred a crippling disease that gradually diminished her bodily movement. Because he loved her dearly and knew she suffered great pain, he restrained himself valiantly from making love to her. One night he was lying beside her, trying to go to sleep, when he felt the bed shaking. Listening for a moment he heard muffled sobs. "Honey, why are you crying?" She hesitantly replied, "Because I don't think you love me any more."

Naturally he was amazed. "What have I done?"

"It's what you haven't done," she wailed. "You don't make love to me anymore."

At first he inwardly responded, "Good grief! What greater affirmation of my love than to deny myself what every organ in my body is crying out for?" But then he realized that his suffering wife desperately needed the reassurance of his love through the act of marriage. All women do.

3. *It satisfies her sex drive.* Although a woman may not possess as strong or consistent a sex drive as a man, she does have a sex drive. Research indicates that almost all women are more passionate just before, during, or after their monthly menstruation and, of course, in the middle of her month at the time of highest fertility. Moreover, her sexual pleasure grows through the years. As she learns to be uninhibited in her responses to her

husband and increasingly learns to experience orgasm, her appreciation and desire for the experience grows.

A woman does not seem so readily tempted to fantasize as does her husband. However, she does have the capacity to remember romantically those exciting experiences of the past. Consequently each thrilling lovemaking event increases her sex drive, in the same way that each frustrating experience stifles it. Such a growing sex drive needs an outlet, and married love is God's ordained plan for its expression.

4. *It relaxes her nervous system.* We have consistently noted that frigid women are nervous women. Note that we did *not* say that every nervous woman is frigid, for some women are simply nervous by nature. But frigidity almost invariably produces nervousness. It is important, therefore, that a wife learn healthy sexual expression toward her husband.

As with a man, the female nervous system is intrinsically tied to the reproductive organs. God has made it possible for wives from all walks of life to enjoy a hygienically relaxing experience on their marriage bed. The act of marriage exists for the propagation of the race and personal enjoyment, it is true, and it does promote fidelity and fulfillment; but it also contributes a much needed relaxant to the nervous system.

5. *The ultimate experience.* When properly consummated to orgasm, married love provides a woman with life's most exciting experience. One young mother took exception to that statement, insisting that childbearing offered greater excitement. But we refer to a feminine experience on a regular and frequent basis. There is simply no experience comparable to the act of marriage — for both the wife and the husband — who need each other to gain its ultimate rewards.

THE MOST BEAUTIFUL MEANING OF ALL

An important meaning for the act of marriage is

purposely presented last. We think it is the most beautiful of all. Simply stated, it is the provision of one ongoing life experience that a husband and wife share uniquely with each other. In all life's other activities we are compelled to share each other. If the husband is a teacher or mechanic, other persons share in the fruits of his skills. If the wife is a good cook or an attractive woman, the husband is not the only one who enjoys those gifts. But behind their closed bedroom door, a couple experiences oneness — a sublime moment uniting them in an exclusively intimate union unshared by anyone else on earth. That is a major reason why the act of marriage is such a binding, uniting, and enriching influence on a couple.

The meaning of oneness resulting from mutual lovemaking is far more important than the time spent in the experience. If a typical couple spends about thirty minutes in a single lovemaking experience an average of three times a week, the act of love would account for only 1½ hours per week, or nine-tenths of 1 percent of their time. Yet no other repeatable experience is more important to that couple. The partners who relate enjoyably to each other spend many hours in emotional and mental harmony in anticipation of the experience and follow it with many hours of mutual contentment and closeness because of their love. Probably no powerful human encounter cements their relationship more firmly than the act of marriage.

Notes

[1] Jerome Rainer and Julie Rainer, *Sexual Pleasure in Marriage* (New York: Pocket Books, 1959), p. 30.

3

For Women Only

One outstanding observation gleaned from my years in the counseling room is that women enjoy a greater capacity for love than do men, a capacity that includes both giving and receiving. For this reason it seems women usually try harder than men to be good and faithful lovers. One thing has been obvious — far more women than men are willing to settle for a second-rate love life. Fortunately neither must endure such a condition any longer.

It is vitally important to a married woman's self-acceptance that her husband be satisfied with her as a love partner. One loving wife with a self-acceptance rating of zero lamented, "My husband thinks I'm an ideal cook, homemaker, and mother for his children, but he left me because I was a failure in the bedroom." Most men will accept mediocrity in other areas if the bedroom activity gives satisfaction. We have regularly noticed that nearly every wife genuinely wants to succeed in this important area of marriage, but too many just don't know how to proceed. Therefore some suggestions directed specifically to wives will be helpful.

1. *Maintain a positive mental attitude*. When en

route to Hawaii with my wife for a few days' vacation before a seminar, I was reading Marabel Morgan's book, *The Total Woman.* Beverly was startled when I suddenly started to laugh, but her response was identical when I showed her the cause. Mrs. Morgan indicated that the brain is the control center in women for making love. I had long been aware of that fact, but was astounded to find a woman who would admit it.

Proverbs 23:7 reminds us, "For as he thinketh in his heart, so is he." Students of the mind are discovering that a person never rises above his expectations. When a person anticipates failure, he will never succeed. If, however, he expects success, he will achieve it. For the woman concerned about lovemaking success, talent, I.Q., and age have little to do with it; her mental attitude is the determining factor. We all have observed people who outperform their natural capabilities. It is our conviction that every Christian, empowered by the Holy Spirit, should outperform his own natural abilities in whatever situation he finds himself.

As a counselor I have been surprised by the number of beautiful women, the embodiment of sexual appeal, who confess that they are completely inept in the bedroom. On the other hand, some "plain Janes," flatchested or overweight, admit to an exciting love life with their husbands. This proves that it isn't primarily the size, shape, or appearance of a woman that makes her a good lover; it suggests that her mental attitude is of utmost importance.

Three areas in a woman's sexual thinking pattern are very important to her: (a) what she thinks about lovemaking; (b) what she thinks about herself; and (c) what she thinks about her husband. Her attitude toward these will determine her success or failure.

(a) *What she thinks about lovemaking.* Although we cannot endorse the sexual revolution, it may be somewhat responsible for exposing the false concept that married love is "dirty," "evil," or "for masculine enjoyment only."

Such impressions certainly did not emanate from the Old or New Testament or from the early church. They sprang from the "Dark Ages" when Roman theologians tried to merge ascetic philosophy with Christian thought. The pagan philosophy that assumed that anything enjoyable must be evil took precedence over the biblical concept that "Marriage is honourable in all, and the bed undefiled" (Heb. 13:4). It is difficult to describe some of the unbelievable and ridiculous distortions to which the sacred relationship of married love has been subjected. One author wrote,

> Peter Lombard and Gratien warned Christians that the Holy Spirit left the room when a married couple engaged in sexual intercourse — even if it were for the purpose of conceiving a child! Other church leaders insisted that God required sexual abstinence during all holy days and seasons. And in addition, couples were advised not to have sex relations on Thursdays in honor of Christ's arrest, on Fridays in memory of His crucifixion, on Saturdays in honor of the Virgin Mary, on Sundays in remembrance of Christ's resurrection, and on Mondays out of respect for the departed souls (leaving only Tuesday and Wednesday)! The Church sought to regulate every facet of life, leaving no room for the individual's right to determine God's will, nor for the rights of a married couple to decide for themselves how the most intimate aspects of married life should be conducted.[1]

The Reformation fortunately called Christians back to studying the Word of God rather than blindly accepting dogma. In gaining new insights into God, salvation, sin, and theology, Christians discovered that God is the author of sex, that both men and women have sexual needs which a partner is obliged to fulfill (1 Cor. 7:1-5), and that their fulfillment is honorable and undefiled. Obedient Christians over the centuries have discovered in the privacy of their bedrooms that sexual relations provide the most exciting experiences in their lives. Any young woman who enters marriage without knowing it is a blessing from her heavenly Father, to be enjoyed without reserve, does not fully understand the Bible.

Confused church leaders of the past are not the only ones who seemed to delight in warping the mental attitudes of young virgins just prior to marriage. Some communities reported little old ladies who were self-appointed evangelists of frigidity and took it upon themselves to visit the brides-to-be before their weddings to inform them of the "facts of life." Their version was something like this: "S-- is the worst part of marriage. It is distasteful and disgusting but something every wife must endure." By the time the "evangelist" was through, no young virgin could possibly anticipate the joys of married love. Such sexual misfits are contagious. Having never welcomed the experience, they feel dutybound to keep anyone else from enjoying it.

One frigid wife told this story in the counseling room. About two weeks before her marriage, her Aunt Matilda caught her and psychologically marred her for the first five years of marriage. Apparently her aunt, whose marriage was arranged by her parents in the old country, found herself petrified of sex on her wedding night. When her embarrassed and clumsy farmer husband, who was twenty years older, brought her to their wedding bed, he "stripped me naked and raped me in my own bed. I fought and screamed to no avail. My virginity was gone and I cried for three days. I have hated sex faithfully for thirty-five years." Her conclusion to her niece was, "As far as I'm concerned, marriage is just legalized rape."

As much as one might feel compassion for poor Aunt Matilda and her equally unhappy spouse, we can hardly envision more unhealthy concepts to pump into the impressionable young mind of a bride-to-be. It is little wonder that it took her niece several years and several counseling experiences to overcome such disastrous ideas.

How much better it would be for the young bride if

her mother, whose love relationship for her husband had been accepted by their children through the years, would share with her that married love is beautiful, exciting, meaningful, and mutually enjoyable. Such young virgins are mentally fortified against the false notions of Aunt Matilda and rarely become frigid women.

The following illustration clarifies that a woman's mental attitude is the key to the use of her sexual apparatus. After listening for an hour as a couple, who had come for counseling, discussed their miserable sex life, I excused the husband for a few minutes in order to ask the woman why they made love only two or three times a month. The wife reported, "I'm not as robust as most women; I think my female organs are too small, and I can't function like other women." (Modern research indicates that all female organs, like those of their male counterparts, are approximately the same size regardless of the person's size.) When she admitted to suffering from arthritis, I shared with her some information that I had recently read reporting that tension accentuated pain in arthritis patients. Inasmuch as marital relations are a God-given means of relaxing emotional tensions, I counseled her to try more frequent lovemaking to help ease her arthritic pains. One week later I received a frantic phone call from her husband. "I don't know what you told my wife after I left the room, but she has made love to me seven times in the last seven days — and I'm not sure I can keep up with this pace!"

What turned the wife on? I suggested no medication, vitamins, or mechanical devices — merely a change in her mental attitude, the most powerful tool in combating sexual dysfunction.

(b) *What she thinks about herself.* Self-rejection is one of the most common maladies of our day. Men fret about their penes being too small or too soft; women worry about having miniature-sized breasts or being undersexed. Actually, the percentage of sexually normal people is enormous. In fact, tests have proved that "undersized" people (whatever that is supposed to mean) are just as responsive or sensitive sexually as anyone else — and sometimes more so.

Anxiety over one's ability to function sexually is the primary cause of sexual malfunction. Researchers report that men have functioned normally after various parts of their reproductive systems were removed, such as testicles or prostate glands. Interestingly enough, women who have had their clitorises removed for some reason reported no adverse effect on their sexual capability, and many women indicate increased marital enjoyment after having a hysterectomy. From all the evidence we must conclude that the organs themselves are not of primary importance, but what we think about them — and ourselves. If we regard ourselves as sexually expressive and responsive love partners, we are — or at least have that capability.

(c) *What she thinks about her husband.* "I can't stand to have my husband touch me!" Thus began the mother of five who had become infatuated with another man. She confessed, "Ten minutes to five is the most miserable time of my day because as I stand at the sink, getting dinner ready, I know that Tom will be home in ten minutes and will kiss me when he comes in."

After we seriously dealt with her mental love affair with a divorced man as a sin, Julie got down on her knees and confessed her sins through her tears. Two weeks later my phone rang at 4:55 P.M. and Julie reported excitedly, "God has changed my heart! I'm all dressed up, excited that Tom is due home in a few minutes. I called because I wanted you to know that this has now become the most exciting time of my day."

Love is not a whimsical vapor that comes and goes without rhyme or reason. It is a vital emotion that grows or dies in direct proportion to one's thinking pattern. If a person gripes and criticizes his partner in his mind, before long his love will die. If, however, that negative mental habit is replaced by thanksgiving for the positive characteristics in a partner's life, love will blossom as surely as night follows day. "But let us, who are of the day, be sober, putting on the breastplate of faith and love; and for an helmet, the hope of salvation" (1 Thess. 5:8). Love is the result of thinking wholesome thoughts about one's partner. "Finally, brethren, whatsoever things are true, whatsoever things are honest, whatsoever things are just, whatsoever things are pure, whatsoever things are lovely, whatsoever things are of good report; if there be any virtue, and if there be any praise, think on these things" (Phil. 4:8). Many times we have seen love return to a marriage when one or both were willing to obey the principle, "In every thing give thanks: for this is the will of God in Christ Jesus concerning you" (1 Thess. 5:18).

A couple came to my office as a last resort. They told me, "We have an appointment with our attorney on Thursday to get a divorce." It was then Tuesday. "Is there anything you can do to bring love back into our marriage before it is too late? We have three children."

"No, there is nothing I can do," I responded, "but I know Someone who can." They quickly admitted to being Christians but added that they "hadn't worked at it lately." I explained, "God commands married couples to love one another, and He never demands that we do anything for which He will not provide the strength." They remained dubious.

Sensing their spirit of hopelessness, I offered a quiet word of prayer for instruction and found myself asking, "How would you like to fall madly in love with each other again in three weeks' time?" They brightened at the thought, but doubted it was possible. I began to share with them that criticism, nitpicking, faultfinding, and griping in our minds is destructive of love (and verbalizing those feelings is even worse). I further stressed that God condemns such thinking, commanding us instead to think with love and thanksgiving about everything. Taking two three-by-five cards from my desk, I turned to the husband

and asked him to list ten things about his wife that he liked. The first items took a while, but soon the others flowed out. When the wife's turn came to list his good points, it was easier, for she had been planning her list as he proceeded with his.

When their lists were complete, they agreed to review them every morning and night and thank God for each of those blessings. Within three weeks they called to break their next appointment, saying, "We don't need any more counseling; our love has returned stronger than before."

If your love has become stagnant, your mind is the culprit. Try mental praise; it will change your life.

2. *Relax! Relax! Relax!* It should come as no surprise that a virgin will be rather tense in anticipation of her first intercourse. Why shouldn't she be? Every new experience produces nervous excitement — it's perfectly normal. But like anything else in life, repetition leads to relaxation. It is vitally important that a wife learn to relax in the act of marriage, for all bodily functions operate better under such conditions.

This need for relaxation may be illustrated in a woman's production of vaginal lubrication. Almost all women have the glands necessary to produce this needed fluid that makes possible the entrance of the penis without pain. But when she is tense or nervous, the glands will not function adequately, and she will experience some friction that may be painful. Actually the very fear of that pain can restrict the normal flow of fluids the next time.

Most counselors recommend using a lubricating vaginal jelly during the first few weeks of marriage, which will eliminate the probability of pain and help attain more relaxation. The less tension in the wife, the easier her reproductive organs cooperate with her in the accomplishment of an orgasm.

A wife's relaxation is important to her loving husband, because if he senses that she is tense or afraid, he may interpret that to signify her fear of him. Her relaxation inspires his own.

3. *Chuck your inhibitions.* Though modesty is an admirable virtue in a woman, it is out of place in the bedroom with her husband. The Bible teaches that Adam and Eve in their unfallen state were "naked and not ashamed" (Gen. 2:25). Frankly speaking, that means that even in their nakedness they were uninhibited. It may take time for a chaste woman to shake off the inhibitions of her premarriage days and learn to be open with her husband — but it is absolutely essential.

An attractive couple requested guidance for what they called "sexual frustration." The wife of twelve years was too embarrassed to let her husband watch her disrobe at night. "My mother taught me that good women never do that kind of thing," she explained.

I responded, "Just because your mother made the lifetime mistake of failing to make her husband and your father an exception to her modest standards, there is no reason for you to perpetuate that error." I suggested that she let her husband help her undress and encouraged her to relax and enjoy it. It took a while, for she even felt guilty when she found it exciting; but gradually she overcame her acute reticence.

4. *Remember that men are stimulated by sight.* Our Lord said, "Whosoever looketh on a woman to lust after her hath committed adultery with her already in his heart" (Matt. 5:28). Has it ever occurred to you that He made no such directive concerning a woman lusting after a man? The reason is clear. Men are quickly stimulated visually, and the most beautiful object in a man's world is a woman.

Many women counselors urge wives to make the daily homecoming of their husbands the most significant time of the day. By bathing, fixing their hair, and putting on fresh attire, they are prepared to give their husbands an enthusiastic welcome home each night. A contented husband is one who is assured that the loveliest sight of

55

the day greets him when he opens the door at night.

Some women resent making their husband's homecoming the object of such attention. Others greet prince charming in their work clothes and curlers in an attempt to impress him with the grievous nature of their daily chores with "his kids." The sight of a bedraggled wife may engender sympathy (though it's doubtful), but it will rarely inspire love. A woman has more assets than she thinks, so she might as well take advantage of them. "Clean up, paint up, fix up" is a good motto for every loving wife to remember just before the time of hubby's arrival. We have observed that the women who go that extra mile seem to avoid the problem of "How can I get my husband to be content to come home at night and spend the evening with the family?" If he is provided with a good reason to come home, he usually will.

5. *Never nag, criticize, or ridicule.* Since we have already noted that most young men are insecure and desperately need the loving approval of their wives, we will not belabor the point here. Nevertheless, it is important to remember that nothing turns a man off faster than motherly nagging and criticism or ridicule of his manhood. No matter how upset a wife may become, she should never stoop to such conduct, or she may jeopardize a beautiful relationship.

A brilliant doctor with a beautiful, cultured wife had an affair with a woman who had almost no education and was not nearly so attractive as his wife. In fact, he admitted that she was not as sexually enjoyable as his wife. When asked to explain his behavior, he replied, "She makes me feel comfortable." Upon reflection, his wife realized that she had gradually become very critical of his actions and nagged him about the long hours he spent at the office. Not being gifted with ready speech, he had responded by staying away in pursuit of a haven of peace. The other woman was the way he found a little peace and quiet he had longed for.

6. *Remember that you are a responder.* God placed

within the feminine heart the amazing ability to respond to her husband. Most women admit to having exciting experiences they would never otherwise have attempted except in response to something initiated by their husbands. This is particularly true of their love lives.

Except for those occasions when a wife is particularly amorous and initiates lovemaking, the husband makes the first approach most of the time. Since men are quickly stimulated visually, on many occasions a husband will approach his wife with amorous intentions when lovemaking is farthest from her mind. The nature of her response often determines the outcome. If she reacts with a sign of indifference (perhaps a groan or yawn), it will probably end right there. On the other hand, if she cuddles close to him for a few minutes and accepts his advances, however passively at first, she will gradually find her mood beginning to match his as her own motor of amorousness ignites.

Many a wife has cheated herself and her husband out of countless lovemaking experiences because she did not understand the unique responding ability of a woman.

7. *Observe daily feminine hygiene*. When Beverly was in high school, her girls' physical education instructor told the class that men have a stronger sense of smell than women. That made such an impression on her as a teenager that she has always been exceedingly careful in this matter.

Whether that girls' coach was right I do not know, but every woman must be careful of body odors for two reasons: first, in some women the vaginal fluids, especially those which have dried on the outside, can emit a strong odor unless she bathe regularly; and second, she may become immune to her own body smells. In this day of various special soaps, lotions, and deodorants, body odors should never be a problem.

8. *Communicate freely*. One of a woman's biggest sexual misconceptions is that her husband knows all about sex. That is rarely, if ever, true. Men may be interested in

the subject from the day after they graduate from kindergarten, but they may also be too embarrassed to go to the right sources for the proper information. To complicate the problem, men can be notorious liars whenever they discuss the subject of sex.

As an eighteen-year-old in the air force, I listened with fascination to the "big boys" tell of their sexual exploits. When those old stories come back to mind now, I have to smile. Most of them were either lies or exaggerations, for many of them were impossible.

Unless a man has read the right books or sought knowledge in the right places, much of what he thinks about women is likely wrong when he enters marriage. The wife should not feel discouraged about this; she should look on this as an exciting opportunity to inform him about the one woman in the world whom he should know intimately. She must learn to communicate freely. Besides telling him how she feels, she should guide his hands to show him what gives her pleasure. Unless she tells him what excites her, he may never know. A wife will probably have to teach only one man in her lifetime about her intimate self. She should do it thoroughly and make it an exciting experience, rewarding to both her and her husband.

9. *When all else fails, pray.* That may sound strange for a minister to say, but if you understand my meaning, I think you'll consider it a valid suggestion. I am convinced that God never intended any Christian couple to spend a lifetime in the sexual wilderness of orgasmic malfunction. He has placed within every woman the sexual capabilities which He meant for her to enjoy. His only real prohibition relates to their use outside of marriage. When kept within the confines of that sacred institution, these capabilities should provide mutual pleasure for both partners. If it isn't a pleasurable experience, He has something better in store for you, so pray about it and expect Him to direct you to an adequate solution. "Hitherto have ye asked nothing in my name:

ask, and ye shall receive, that your joy may be full" (John 16:24).

Notes

[1] Letha Scanzoni, *Sex and the Single Eye* (Grand Rapids: Zondervan Publishing House, 1968), p. 31.

Bibliography

Andelin, Aubrey P. *Man of Steel and Velvet*. Santa Barbara, Calif.: Pacific Press Santa Barbara, 1972.

Anthony, Catherine Parker. *Textbook of Anatomy and Physiology*. St. Louis: C. V. Mosby Co., 1963.

Bird, Lewis P., and Reilly, Christopher T. *Learning to Love*. Waco, Tex.: Word Books, 1971.

Caprio, Frank S. *Sex and Love*. New York: The Citadel Press, 1965.

————. *The Sexually Adequate Male*. Greenwich, Conn.: Fawcett Publications, 1951.

Chandler, Sandra S. *The Sensitive Woman*. Pasadena: Compass Press, 1972.

Clark, LeMon. *101 Intimate Sexual Problems Answered*. New York: New American Library, 1968.

Cooke, Charles E., and Ross, Eleanore. *Sex Can Be an Art!* Los Angeles: Sherbourne Press, 1964.

Curtis, Lindsay R. *Sensible Sex* (A Guide for Newlyweds). San Juan, Puerto Rico: Searle & Co., 1971.

Deutsch, Ronald M. *The Key to Feminine Response in Marriage*. New York: Random House, 1968.

Drakeford, John W. *The Great Sex Swindle*. Nashville: Broadman Press, 1966.

Ellzey, W. Clark. *How to Keep Romance in Your Marriage*. New York: Association Press, 1965.

Florio, Anthony. *Two to Get Ready*. Old Tappan, N.J.: Fleming H. Revell Co., 1974.

Greenblat, Bernard R. *A Doctor's Marital Guide for Patients*. Chicago: Budlong Press, 1964.

Hamilton, Eleanor. *Sex Before Marriage*. New York: Meredith Press, 1969.

Jones, H. Kimball. *Toward a Christian Understanding of the Homosexual*. New York: Association Press, 1966.

Levin, Robert, and Levin, Amy. "Sexual Pleasure: The

Surprising Preferences in 100,000 Women." *Red-book* 145 (September, 1970).

Masters, William H., and Johnson, Virginia E. *Human Sexual Response*. Boston: Little, Brown and Co., 1966.

Miles, Herbert J. *Sexual Happiness in Marriage*. Grand Rapids: Zondervan Publishing House, 1967.

Mumford, Bob. *Living Happily Ever After*. Old Tappan, N.J.: Fleming H. Revell Co., 1973.

Petersen, J. Allan, ed. *The Marriage Affair*. Wheaton, Ill.: Tyndale House Publishers, 1971.

Piper, Otto A. *The Biblical View of Sex and Marriage*. New York: Charles Scribner's Sons, 1960.

Rainer, Jerome, and Rainer, Julia. *Sexual Pleasure in Marriage*. New York: Pocket Books, 1959.

Reuben, David. *Any Woman Can!* New York: David McKay Co., 1971.

_____. *Everything You Always Wanted to Know About Sex*. New York: David McKay Co., 1969.

_____. *How to Get More Out of Sex.* New York: David McKay Co., 1974.

Rice, Shirley. *The Christian Home: A Woman's View*. Norfolk: Norfolk Christian Schools, 1965.

_____. *Physical Unity in Marriage: A Woman's View*. Norfolk: Norfolk Christian Schools, 1973.

Robinson, Marie N. *The Power of Sexual Surrender*. New York: New American Library, 1962.

Scanzoni, Letha. *Sex and the Single Eye*. Grand Rapids: Zondervan Publishing House, 1968.

_____. *Sex Is a Parent Affair*. Glendale, Calif.: Gospel Light Publications, 1973.

Sheridan, Edward P., and Sheridan, Kathleen, eds. *28 Experts View the Sexual Marriage*. Huntington, Ind.: Our Sunday Visitor, 1974.

Smith, Bob. *Love Story . . . the Real Thing*. Staff research at Peninsula Bible Church, Palo Alto, Calif., 1974.

Strong, James. "Dictionary of the Words in the Greek Testament" in *Strong's Exhaustive Concordance of*

Words in the Greek Testament. New York: Abingdon-Cokesbury Press, 1890.

Subak-Sharpe, Genell J. "Is Your Sex Life Going Up in Smoke?" *Reader's Digest*, 106 (January, 1975).

Thayer, Joseph Henry. *Thayer's Greek-English Lexicon of the New Testament*. Marshalltown, Del.: National Foundation for Christian Education, 1885, revised edition, 1889.

Timmons, Tim. *One Plus One*. Washington, D.C.: Canon Press, 1974.

Vincent, M.O. *God, Sex and You*. Philadelphia: J.B. Lippincott Co., 1970.